WHAT DO WE KNOW ABOUT URANUS?

Astronomy for Beginners
Children's Astronomy & Space Books

BABY PROFESSOR

EDUCATION KIDS

Uranus is a part of our solar system and is the seventh planet away from the Sun. Our solar system is beautiful and amazing. Read further to learn about this planet.

URANUS SPECIFICATIONS

Uranus has 21 moons (and more to come in the future) and is 14.5 times the Earth's mass size. Its diameter is 31,763 miles and one year on Uranus is 83.8 years on Earth. It is two times as far away from the Sun as Saturn is.

Its day lasts for 17.2 hours and its temperature is -280 degrees Fahrenheit (that's cold!). It is the seventh planet away from the sun, a distance of 1.8 billion miles. It is an ice giant which means its surface is comprised of gas and its interior is composed of rock and ice. Uranus is the coldest and largest of all the planets of our Solar System.

Its surface consists mostly of hydrogen gas as well as some helium gas. 25% of its atmosphere is comprised of gas.

Its atmosphere can be stormy, but not as active or stormy as Jupiter or Saturn. Because of this, its surface is fairly uniform and featureless.

Uranus is the solar system's third largest planet. It contains about 63 times the volume of Earth. What this means is if Uranus was hollow, 63 Earths would be able to fit inside of it. It has 16 times the amount of surface area as Earth has and is 14.5 times as massive. Can you imagine how big that is?

THE MOONS OF URANUS

As mentioned earlier, it has 27 known moons. It also has 9 irregular moons, 5 major moons, and 13 inner moons. All of these moons are named for characters in William Shakespeare's plays.

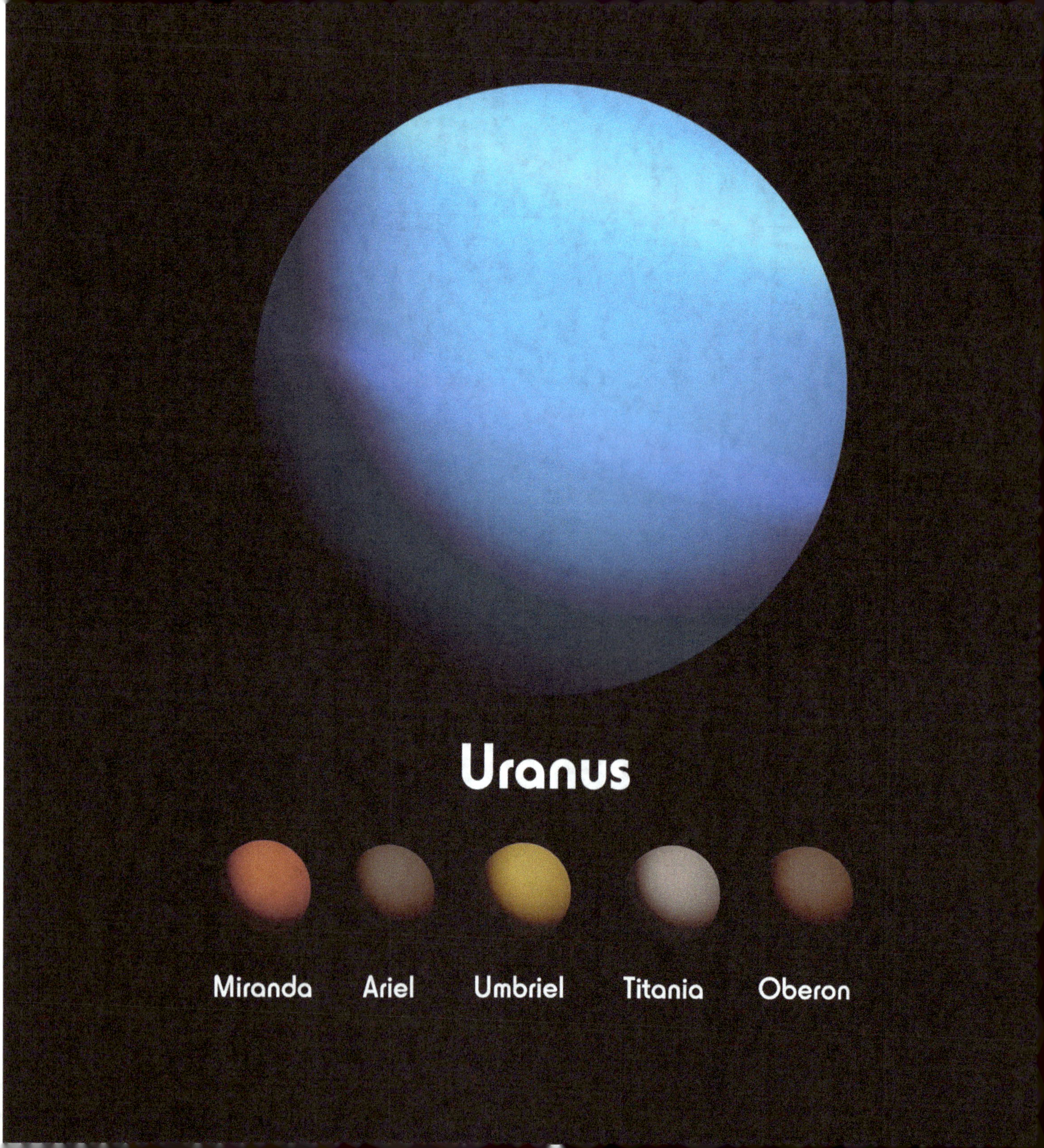
Uranus
Miranda
Ariel
Umbriel
Titania
Oberon

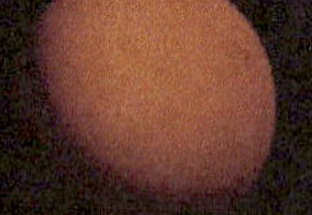

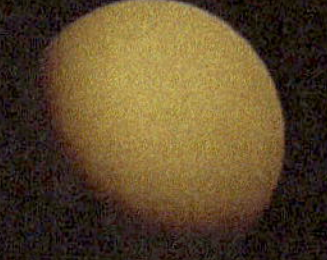

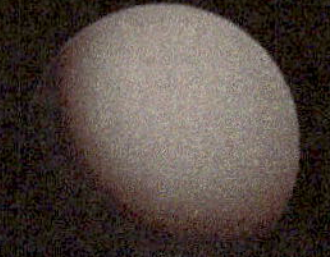

The largest one is Titania, which is named for a character in A Midsummer's Night Dream, measuring over 900 miles in diameter and it orbits the planet from a distance of approximately 240,000 miles. While it is only approximately five percent as massive as Earth's moon, it's the 8th largest moon of the solar system.

WHAT DOES IT LOOK LIKE?

Uranus is bright bluish-green in color which is a result of the methane contained in its atmosphere. You should be able to view it with only your naked eyes.

Uranus has rings also, although they do not stretch out as far as Saturn's rings. There are thirteen known rings, primarily composed of small particles that may be remnants of a fragmented moon. All of these rings are quite narrow, with all of them being less than a mile or two wide.

WHY DOES IT TILT ON ITS SIDE?

Uranus rotates on its side, which makes it very unique. If you can envision the Sun and all of the planets on a table, the other planets rotate, similar to a top. On the other hand, Uranus rolls similar to a marble. Scientists believe that this odd rotation is due to Uranus being struck by another huge planetoid object causing this change to its tilt.

CLOUD AND BAND PATTERNS

While it may seem like a boring blue ball since we can't see the clouds and storms like what you might see on Saturn and Jupiter, if you look closer in different wavelengths such as infrared, you can actually see these clouds and band patterns.

In earlier years, there wasn't much to see, but once telescopes were more advanced around the 1990s, they were able to see that it has bright regions contained in its atmosphere. Some clouds will only last for hours, but others have been around since the flyby in 1986 by Voyager. The wind speeds are apparently quite spectacular as well, traveling at a quick pace.

Voyager

IS URANUS SIMILAR TO THE EARTH?

No, in fact it is very much different than the Earth. Since it is a gas giant, which means that its surface is comprised of gas, you cannot even stand up. Since it is so much further away from the Sun, it is much colder than Earth is.

In addition, its strange rotation makes for much different seasons. There would be sunshine on some areas of Uranus for up to 42 years and it would then be dark for 42 years. It is also much bigger that Earth.

URANUS

HOW DID WE FIND OUT ABOUT URANUS?

It was first named as a planet by William Herschel, a British astronomer. He discovered this planet by telescope. Before this discovery by Herschel, scientists thought it was a star. The Voyager 2 is the only space probe that has been sent to Uranus, in 1986, bringing back some detailed pictures of the planet and its rings and moons.

WHAT IS THE MEANING OF ITS NAME?

Uranus was the husband of the Earth and lord of the skies in astronomy mythology. Also, he was king of the gods until being overthrown by Saturn, his son.

It is the only planet that is named for a Greek god instead of a Roman god. Uranus was married to Mother Earth and was the Greek god of the sky.

WHAT WOULD YOU WEIGH ON URANUS?

If you wanted to fly to this planet, it would take many years. Upon arrival, you would weigh less than you do on Earth since Uranus' gravity doesn't have the strength it does on Earth. Because of this different in the pull of gravity, if you weighed 70 pounds (32 kg) on Earth, your weight on Uranus would be 62 pounds (28 kg).

THE SOLAR SYSTEM

The Sun is located at the center of our Solar System. The Solar System consists of all the planets, the asteroids, and any other objects orbiting the Sun.

Mercury
Venus
Earth
Mars
Jupiter
Saturn
Uranus
Neptune
Pluto

Terrestrial Planets

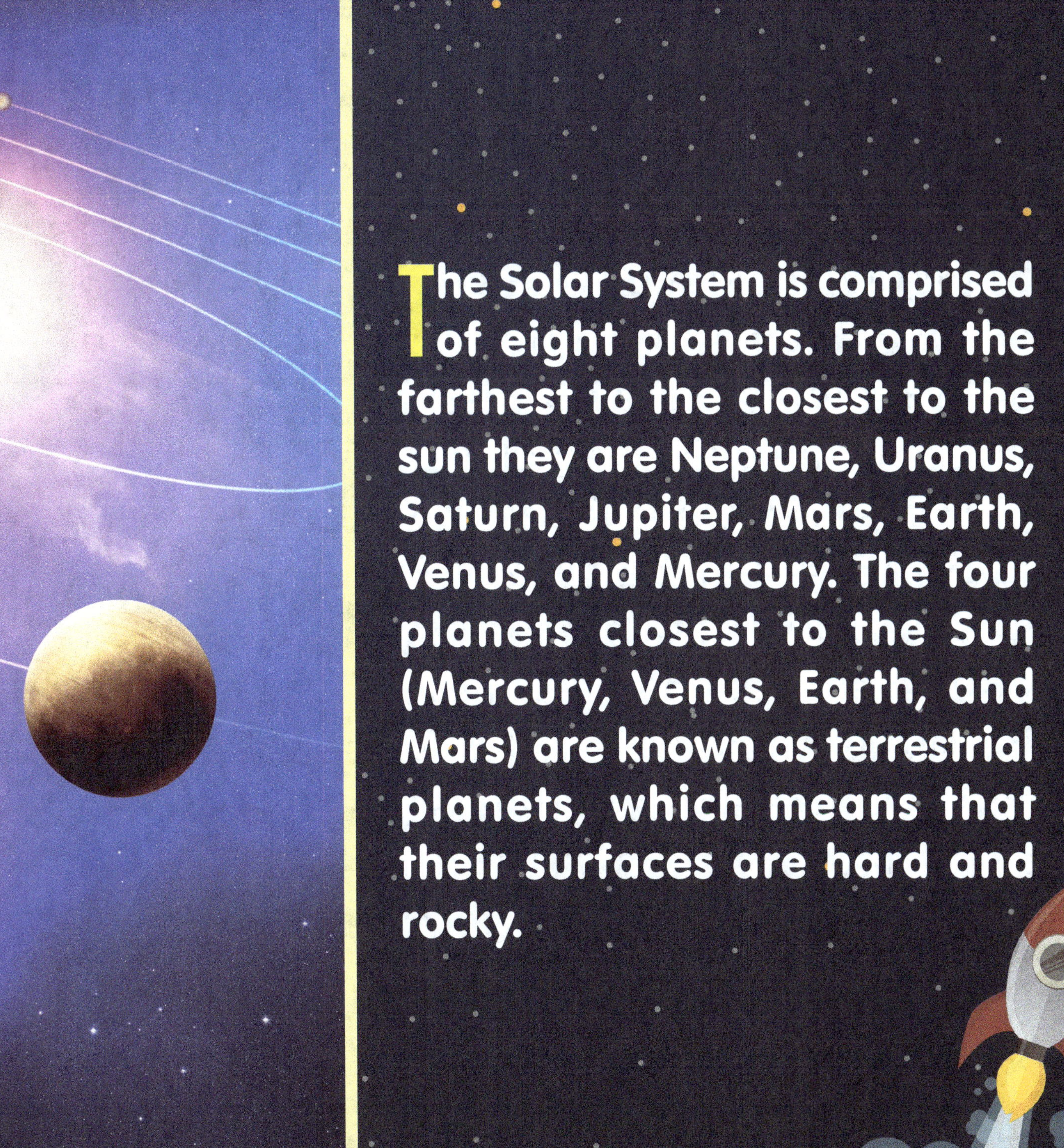

The Solar System is comprised of eight planets. From the farthest to the closest to the sun they are Neptune, Uranus, Saturn, Jupiter, Mars, Earth, Venus, and Mercury. The four planets closest to the Sun (Mercury, Venus, Earth, and Mars) are known as terrestrial planets, which means that their surfaces are hard and rocky.

The four planets that are farthest away (Jupiter, Saturn, Uranus, and Neptune) are referred to as gas giants. They are much larger in size and their surface is made up of gas elements, mostly being hydrogen.

The solar system also consists of other objects in addition to the eight planets and the sun.

Pluto

Dwarf planets – These planets are objects that are similar to the planets in the Solar System. They are, however, defined as not having "cleared their orbital region of other objects." They include Makemake, Haumea, Eris, Ceres and Pluto.

Comets - These are objects consisting of rocks, ice, and dust orbiting the sun. Sometimes they have a visible "tail" of gas that emanates from solar wind and radiation. Comets originate from the Oort cloud and the Kuiper belt.

Asteroid belt – This is a region located between the planets Jupiter and Mars. There are thousands of rocky objects orbiting the sun in this region, ranging in size from tiny dust particles to Ceres, one of the dwarf planets.

Kuiper Belt

Kuiper belt – This is a region made up of thousands of tiny bodies existing outside the orbit of the planets. Ammonia, water, and methane are "ices" which make up the objects in the Kuiper belt.

Oort cloud – This cloud is located quite a bit further out than the Kuiper belt. It is approximately a thousand times as far from the Sun. Until now, scientists have only been able to guess at its existence which they believe consists of thousands of tiny icy objects. It is at the farthest edge of our Solar System.

THE SUN

At the center of the Solar System is a yellow dwarf star known as the Sun, which is surrounded by the planets that orbit it. The Solar System and Sun then orbit around the Milky Way, which is the center of the Galaxy.

While it is relatively a small star among the universe, the Sun is huge amongst the solar system. Even considering the massive gas planets such as Saturn and Jupiter, the Sun has 99.8% of the mass in our solar system.

The Sun consists of helium gas and superheated hydrogen. Approximately 74% of the Sun's mass is made of hydrogen. At its center, the hydrogen atoms that are under excessive pressure from gravity go through a process known as nuclear fusion and are converted to helium atoms. This process creates a great amount of heat that causes radiation and is what eventually ends up as the sunlight we see at Earth.

Sun

Telescope

WHAT IS A TELESCOPE?

Telescopes are instruments that we use to be able to see objects far away. They are often used to view stars and planets. Some technology used in telescopes is used also in cameras and binoculars.

Two more important properties are its light gathering ability and magnification. The better the its ability to gather light, the better you can see faint objects and far away stars in the sky at night. This is typically determined by the size of its aperture, or opening, of the telescope.

The greater the aperture, the more light that can be gathered by the telescope. The magnification describes how much bigger the telescope can make the objects appear.

Each planet of our Solar System is amazing in their own way. It's fun to learn how they orbit the sun and how different each planet is from the others.

Uranus

Now that you have learned about the Planet Uranus and the Solar System, you may have questions about the other planets. For additional information, you can go to your local library, research the internet, and ask questions of your teachers, family and friends.

Visit

BABY PROFESSOR
EDUCATION KIDS

www.BabyProfessorBooks.com
to download Free Baby Professor eBooks and view
our catalog of new and exciting Children's Books

www.ingramcontent.com/pod-product-compliance
Lightning Source LLC
Chambersburg PA
CBHW060137120726
48003CB00009B/2927